juggling

a *flowmotion*™ title

juggling

colin francome

Sterling Publishing Co., Inc.

New York

Created and conceived by
Axis Publishing Limited
8c Accommodation Road
London NW11 8ED
www.axispublishing.co.uk

Creative Director: Siân Keogh
Managing Editor: Brian Burns
Project Designer: Sean Keogh
Project Editor: Antony Atha
Production Manager: Sue Bayliss
Photographer: Mike Good

Library of Congress Cataloguing-in-Publication
Data Available

10 9 8 7 6 5 4 3 2 1

Published in 2002 by Sterling Publishing Co., Inc.
387 Park Avenue South, New York, NY 10016
Text and images © Axis Publishing Limited 2002
Distributed in Canada by Sterling Publishing
c/o Canadian Manda Group,
One Atlantic Avenue, Suite 105
Toronto, Ontario, M6K 3E7, Canada

Separation by United Graphics Pte Limited
Printed and bound by Star Standard (Pte) Limited

Sterling ISBN 0–8069–9368–5

a *flowmotion*™ title

juggling

contents

who can juggle? you can juggle!

People who have watched jugglers performing their smooth, apparently effortless movements have often wondered how difficult it is to do. The good news is that the simplest juggling tricks can be performed by nine out of ten people, many of whom will be able to continue and learn the more difficult routines. I have performed at childrens' parties where even children as young as six and seven years old have participated in elementary juggling routines. So I recommend that you give juggling a try.

ten good reasons to juggle

REDUCE STRESS Many businessmen and women juggle at work to reduce the stress of their day-to-day jobs. You need to make regular smooth movements to juggle, and the concentration required for this blots out many problems that might be bothering people.

IMPROVE CONCENTRATION Juggling requires great concentration, especially when learning new tricks or developing skills. A lack of attention can easily result in dropped props.

GOOD EXERCISE Juggling, especially with clubs, requires energy. Expect to do a great deal of bending and picking up at first (if you are getting backache, try practising over a bed). Juggling is good light exercise that develops different parts of the body, depending on the movements you use. Some people walk or run while juggling. This is called joggling. I have run several marathons juggling and was the first person to juggle with three clubs around the Moscow marathon dressed in a clown's outfit.

JUGGLING IS FUN It is easy to take life too seriously, and juggling adds a fun element. It is light hearted compared to many leisure activities.

JUGGLING IS SOCIABLE Although it can be a singular activity, many people derive great pleasure from juggling with others. Other people can teach you new tricks, monitor your performance or find ways for you to improve your technique. You can also pass to each other, which can make a spectacular sight. Juggling to each other requires co-operation and greater skill than juggling alone.

Juggling is a great way to meet new people. There are various juggling clubs around the country, and juggling conventions are held in both this country and abroad.

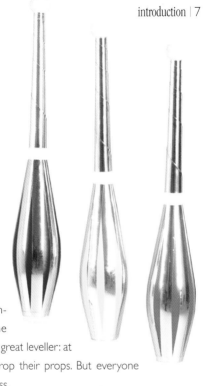

CIGAR BOXES Now part of a juggler's routine, there are lots of tricks you can learn with these. It is better to buy them from a juggler's shop, rather than attempting to fashion your own.

JUGGLING CLUBS These make for a spectacular sight. You can make your own with broom handles and lightweight plastic lemonade bottles, but the specialist clubs found in juggling shops are properly balanced to make catching and throwing easier.

JUGGLING IS INTERNATIONAL Wherever you go and whatever language is spoken, the skill involved in juggling will always be appreciated.

JUGGLERS CAN ENTERTAIN Even if you can only juggle simple patterns with three balls, people will always be amused. In my childrens' show, I introduce a 'naughty ball' that jumps into the air, hides in my arm and jumps into the childrens' arms. Kids find antics like this very amusing.

JUGGLING CAN BE DONE AT ANY TIME If you experience delays while travelling or have some spare time, then you can use it to improve your juggling skills.

SELF IMPROVEMENT

Juggling is essentially non-competitive, with everyone working against gravity. It is a great leveller: at some point everyone will drop their props. But everyone can also improve and progress.

JUGGLING IS NOT COSTLY To begin juggling all you need is three balls, or even three oranges or apples. Many different items lend themselves to juggling, so it is not an expensive hobby to begin. For many years I juggled with tennis balls, which are excellent for bouncing tricks.

famous jugglers

Juggling has a long history. The Greek philosopher Socrates (469–377BC), was said to have attended a banquet where a woman juggled with twelve hoops, although it is doubtful she juggled them all at once. Even the finest modern jugglers, such as Eric Van Aro, have only achieved ten hoops in the air at any one time!

Jugglers were popular in the early Roman Empire. One juggler, Tagatus Ursus, was the first to use glass balls, and other jugglers used lighted torches. In AD347 a female juggler was reported to be using pointed knives. At the time of the Renaissance, mime artists, jesters and jugglers were very popular. Many made a living by travelling from town to town performing their tricks. Around 1770, a French performer called Mathieu Dupois juggled with three apples on a high wire and caught them on the end of forks at the end of his performance. He had a fork in his mouth and one in each hand.

A famous 19th-century juggler called Carl Rappo specialized in devil sticks, and towards the end of the century the development of the music hall led to many jugglers working as entertainers on stage. Some stage jugglers learned tricks from magicians to add to their acts. An Australian juggler called Anglo juggled with lamps, weighted swords and a juggling candle. He wrote a book, *The Art of Modern Juggling*, which was reviewed by the greatest of all magicians and escapologists, Harry Houdini, in March 1908.

A great Italian juggler, Enrico Rastelli was born into a family of jugglers in 1897. He became so successful that by 1925 he was paid £30 a day, then an enormous sum of money. He could juggle eight plates at once, and in one trick spun a ball on his right hand, juggled three sticks with his left, and balanced another stick on his forehead. The celebrated comedian WC Fields began performing with an act as an eccentric tramp juggler. He was unshaven, wore old torn clothing, and was best known for his skill with cigar boxes.

the basic juggling patterns

There are three basic juggling patterns: the cascade, the shower and columns. From these many others follow.

The cascade is the most common pattern used by jugglers and, for most people, it is the easiest to learn. The balls are thrown from side to side across your body, with each throw being made under the incoming ball or club. If the throw is right, the catch will look after itself. You have to be able to catch and throw without looking at the ball or club as it drops towards you.

It is worth spending time to ensure you are throwing accurately. Practise tossing a ball from hand to hand in an easy arc. Throw the ball from about waist height to a point level with the top of your head. Your hands make an inward scooping action so that you can throw the balls under each other. It also prevents them from colliding (kissing) in the air. When you can do this, clap once when the ball is in the air. This will slow down the movement and is a useful way of introducing the next ball.

The next step is to introduce a second ball. Start by holding a ball in each hand. Throw the first ball to your strongest hand. If you are right-handed, throw the left hand ball to your right hand in an arc. As it peaks, throw the right-hand ball in an arc underneath it and catch it in the left hand. Throw each ball to the same height. Many people instinctively pass the second ball across rather than throw it. This would be correct if learning the shower, but does not work for the cascade.

One way of getting the throws right is to throw the balls without attempting to catch them. After a while, practise starting with your other hand. This will help you when you move on to three balls. With the two-ball pattern, there is a space into which you will eventually introduce the third ball. Once you can perform twenty catches successfully with two balls, you can add the third one.

The final step is to hold two balls in your strongest hand and one in the other. The first two throws are just the same as you have practised

JUGGLING BALLS When starting out, use round fruit. Tennis balls are also good, but can be a bit light and bouncy. Beanbags are excellent, as are the slightly larger stage balls. Special silicon juggling balls are the best of all.

with two balls. Choose the hand you are most comfortable holding two balls with. If it is your right, toss one of them towards your left hand. As it peaks throw the ball in your left hand towards the right, and catch the first ball in your left hand. As the second ball peaks, throw the final ball from your right hand before catching the second ball. Keep on repeating this sequence and you are juggling.

The two other patterns are the shower and columns. In the shower the balls follow each other round in a circle. You pass the ball across your body instead of throwing it in the air. In columns you hold the balls in each hand and throw them vertically. The balls do not cross over and you move your hand from side to side to catch and throw.

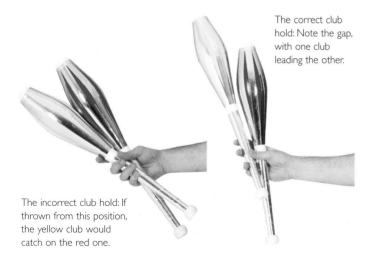

The correct club hold: Note the gap, with one club leading the other.

The incorrect club hold: If thrown from this position, the yellow club would catch on the red one.

JUGGLING TIPS

It's good to remember that very few people manage to juggle at first attempt. If you lack co-ordination, the following tips may be helpful.

● Begin with a warm up session, tossing a single ball from hand to hand.

● Strengthen your weaker hand. If you are right-handed throw the ball against the wall with your left hand. If you stand sideways on to the wall you can mimic the pattern used when you are juggling.

● Some people tend to move forward when they juggle. One way to correct this is to stand in front of a wall when you juggle. Concentrate on throwing the balls at a constant distance from it.

● Take three balls and practise throwing them without trying to catch them. This can help you develop the necessary pattern.

● If you have problems establishing a rhythm or throwing the ball to the correct height, try to relax. Sometimes only patience is needed to develop the necessary skills.

● Beginners often find that the balls smack their hands instead of dropping into them gently. Accentuate your wrist movements so your hand gives a little when you catch the ball.

● Remember that for most of the time only one ball is in the air. Two balls are in the air for only a short time, while one ball is falling into a hand and one is leaving it.

● If you have difficulty juggling three balls, go back to juggling with two and visualise the same move with three balls. You should see a space where the third ball can be inserted.

go with the flow

The special Flowmotion images used in this book have been created to show the whole of each juggling routine using balls, clubs and other objects, such as fruit, hats and plates. Each of these sequences flows across the page from left to right, showing how the balls and other objects are thrown and caught for each operation. Each routine is carefully explained with step-by-step captions flowing from start to finish. Below this, another layer of information is contained in the timeline, breaking the movements into separate moments. These will help you to achieve each stage as you progress. The essence of all successful juggling is accurate throwing and you can only acquire this skill by repeating the throw over and over again until the ball consistently travels along the exact path that you plan for it. Practice makes perfect, so stick with it – juggling is a great activity!

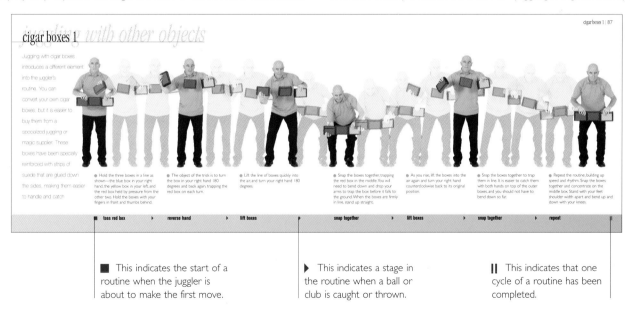

cigar boxes 1 | 87

cigar boxes 1

Juggling with cigar boxes introduces a different element into the juggler's routine. You can convert your own cigar boxes, but it is easier to buy them from a specialized juggling or magic supplier. These boxes have been specially reinforced with strips of suede that are glued down the sides, making them easier to handle and catch.

- Hold the three boxes in a line as shown—the blue box in your right hand, the yellow box in your left, and the red box held by pressure from the other two. Hold the boxes with your fingers in front and thumbs behind.

- The object of the trick is to turn the box in your right hand 180 degrees and back again, trapping the red box on each turn.

- Lift the line of boxes quickly into the air, and turn your right hand 180 degrees.

- Snap the boxes together, trapping the red box in the middle. You will need to bend down and drop your arms to trap the box before it falls to the ground. When the boxes are firmly in line, stand up straight.

- As you rise, lift the boxes into the air again and turn your right hand counterclockwise back to its original position.

- Snap the boxes together to trap them in line. It is easier to catch them with both hands on top of the outer boxes, and you should not have to bend down so far.

- Repeat the routine, building up speed and rhythm. Snap the boxes together and concentrate on the middle box. Stand with your feet shoulder width apart and bend up and down with your knees.

| ■ toss red box | ▶ reverse hand | ▶ lift boxes | ▶ snap together | ▶ lift boxes | ▶ snap together | ▶ repeat | ‖ |

■ This indicates the start of a routine when the juggler is about to make the first move.

▶ This indicates a stage in the routine when a ball or club is caught or thrown.

‖ This indicates that one cycle of a routine has been completed.

juggling with balls

one ball clap

The basis of all juggling is throwing balls, or other objects, up in the air in a pattern and then catching them. You need to establish a rhythm so you make each throw the same as the last: this can only be achieved by practice. This is the first exercise for all would-be jugglers, and is also very useful as a warmup at the start of any routine.

● Start with one ball in your right hand, and stand comfortably with your legs slightly apart, the same width as your hips, Throw the ball in an arc toward your left. The ball should pass cleanly above your head.

● As the ball approaches the top of its arc, clap your hands together. Watch the ball carefully as it moves toward your left. The ball should drop into your hand, which then drops down as you make the catch.

● Toss the ball back toward your right and try to achieve the same arc as before. Make the throw easily so you hand is continuously in motion passing from catch to throw.

● Clap your hands together as the ball passes to your right. Watch the ball carefully at all times, and concentrate on getting a smooth rhythm going from right to left and then left to right.

● You may have to move slightly to catch the ball. Keep your weight balanced evenly on the balls of your feet, and shift slightly from side to side as necessary. As you become better, you will not have to move so much.

● Even if you have had to move to one side to make your catch, keep the same rhythm of throw, clap, catch. Try to throw the ball in a constant arc so the ball always travels along the same path.

● Practice throwing one ball and clapping until you are completely confident that you can repeat the throw time after time. As you improve, the ball will seem to find its way into your hands on its own accord.

throw and clap ▶ **catch and throw** ▶ **clap and catch** ▶ **finish** **11**

The second stage in learning to juggle is to practice with two balls, throwing each ball alternately to left and right. The balls pass each other in the air. Practice throwing the second ball underneath the first, otherwise, they can collide. If you have difficulty getting the timing right, throw the balls without trying to catch them to get the right rhythm.

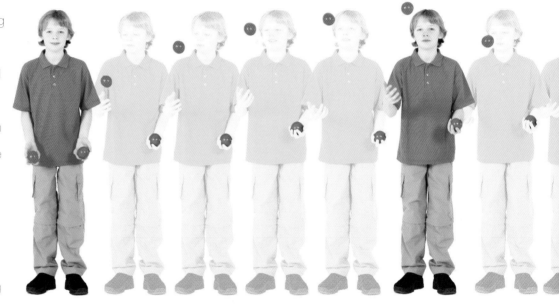

● Start by holding the two balls, one in each hand, standing evenly in the same position as the one ball clap. The red ball will travel to the left and the blue ball to the right. Throw the ball in an easy arc facing ahead.

● The ball should pass just above head height, as shown. Keep your eyes on the ball as it passes above your head toward your left hand.

● The red ball should drop toward your left hand, and as it descends, the blue ball is thrown upward in the same arc to the right. You will need to practice to get the timing right.

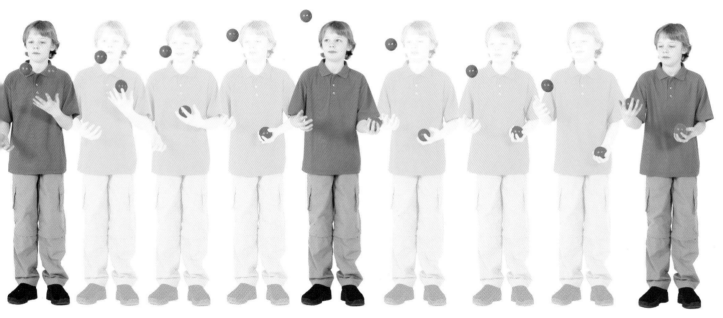

● Raise your left hand as you throw the blue ball, and then let it drop away as you catch the descending red ball. Both hands should move in an easy rhythm as they throw and catch the balls alternately.

● The left hand drops away as the blue ball travels to the right. Keep your eyes on the ball. It should pass just above head height in the same arc as the red ball.

● The blue ball is now traveling toward your right hand that you raise to make the catch. At the beginning, do this quite slowly until you have gained enough confidence to speed up.

● The movement ends with each ball in the opposite hand from the one it started in. You then continue the movement, this time starting with the left hand throwing to the right. Go on repeating this pattern.

catch red ▶ **watch** ▶ **catch blue** ▶ **finish** ‖

three ball cascade

This is probably the most common juggling movement, where the balls appear to cross each other in midair. It is the easiest movement to learn, and many routines can be developed from it. Throw the balls to the same height: do not pass them across from hand to hand.

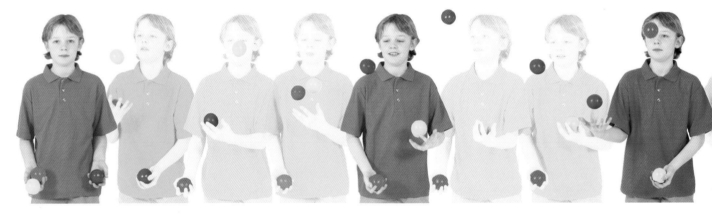

● Start with the red and yellow balls in your right hand and the blue ball in your left hand. Face the front and hold your hands just below waist height.

● Toss the first ball, the yellow one, in an arc toward your left-hand side. The ball should travel as high as the top of your head. As it peaks and starts to fall, bring your left hand in and throw the blue ball under it across to the right.

● Move your left hand out in a circular movement to catch the yellow ball as it falls toward you. Keep your hands moving up and down and in and out. Let your left hand drop as the yellow ball comes into it.

● As the blue ball crosses to your right, repeat the process, throwing the red ball across to the left as the blue ball peaks. Again, bring your right hand in to throw the ball and catch the blue one.

| ■ throw yellow | ▶ | throw blue | ▶ | catch yellow | ▶ | throw red, catch blue | ▶ |

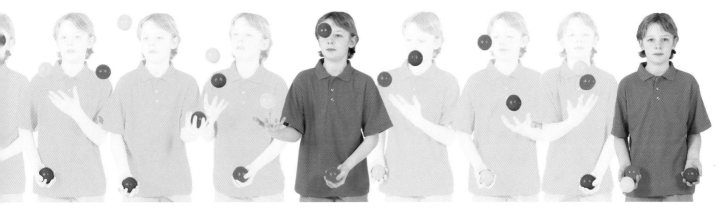

● The red ball now crosses over to the left, and the yellow one is thrown back to the right. Generally speaking, only one ball is high in the air at any one time, with the others entering or leaving your hands.

● Keep the movement rhythmical and regular. Practice until you can throw each ball in a consistent arc. The yellow ball is now dropping to the right, while the blue ball is thrown to the left.

● As the blue ball drops, the red ball is thrown from your left hand. The balls appear to cross each other each time in midair. The trick is to keep your hands moving in a circular motion, throwing each ball under the other.

● To finish your routine, catch two balls in your right hand, holding the third ball in your left. Always face the front, and keep your eyes on the balls in the air as they travel from side to side across your body.

throw yellow, catch red ▶ **throw blue, catch yellow** ▶ **throw red, catch blue** ▶ **finish**

The difference between the reverse cascade and the normal cascade is that you move your hands outward to throw the ball, and the throw is made over the incoming ball and not under it. Your hands move with an outward scoop. The balls will be thrown higher, but avoid throwing them wider, they should be caught close to your body. Keep the movement as controlled as possible.

● Start with the orange and yellow balls in your right hand and the red ball in your left. Throw the orange ball across to your left. As it peaks, throw the red ball up and over the incoming orange ball.

● As you catch the orange ball in your left hand, move your right hand in an outward scoop to throw the yellow ball up and over the incoming orange ball. Catch the red ball close to your body as shown.

● The red ball is now in your right hand while the yellow ball is traveling to your left. Move your left hand out to throw the orange ball over the incoming yellow ball.

■ **throw orange** ▶ **scoop outward** ▶ **throw orange** ▶

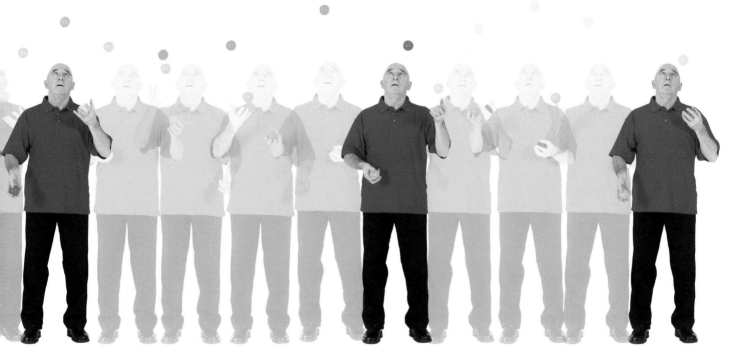

● Throw the balls fairly high. Keep your weight evenly balanced on your feet, and watch the balls in the air. Do not look down. Here the yellow ball has just been caught. Note how close it is to your body.

● Vary your routine by throwing the occasional ball higher in the air. Here the red ball has been thrown higher, with the orange ball being caught by your right hand. See how the hand drops to make the catch.

● Once you have caught the incoming ball, move your hand up and then out in a scooping motion. With practice this will become completely automatic.

● Notice that each throw follows the same arc and your body remains still and in the same position. Finish the routine by catching two balls in your right hand.

catch yellow ▶ **catch orange** ▶ **scoop outward** ▶ **finish** II

two ball column

When you juggle in columns, the balls rise up and down parallel to each other instead of crossing each other in the air. There are three techniques used for this: the inward scoop, the outward scoop, and the straight column, where the juggler's hand moves in a horizontal plane to catch and throw each ball as it rises and falls. This is the movement shown here.

● Start by holding two balls in your right hand and throw the first ball, the blue one, straight up into the air. It can be thrown quite high, as shown. Practice until you can get the ball to follow a straight path up and down.

● As the blue ball drops, throw the yellow ball into the air just to its right. Move your hand to the right to carry out this movement.

● Then move your hand slightly inward, to your left, to catch the .blue ball. Catch the ball by your chest, and then let your arm relax with your hand dropping to your waist. This will help you to catch the ball safely.

■ **throw blue** ▶   **throw, catch** ▶   **throw blue** ▶

● The blue ball is then thrown up parallel to the yellow ball on its way down. Your hand moves out slightly to catch the yellow ball. Keep your eyes fixed firmly on the ball in the air, and watch its path as shown.

● Catch the yellow ball and then throw it up again. Stand with your legs hip width apart so the weight of your body is evenly balanced on your feet.

● When you have established a good rhythm, you can vary the routine by throwing the occasional ball much higher in the air. This adds to the excitement.

● To finish your routine, catch both balls in the same hand. This needs practice. When you are competent with your right hand, start practicing with your left until you can juggle competently with both.

throw, catch orange ▶ **throw orange** ▶ **throw, catch blue** ▶ **finish** II

three ball column with cut across

When you have mastered the two ball column, the next stage is to start juggling with three balls, two in your right hand and one in your left. Normally, the two balls are thrown as described on pages 22–23, with the third ball thrown from the left hand in time with the second ball thrown from your right hand. There are a number of variations to this; the cut across is one of them.

● Throw the first ball, the yellow one, into the air, and hold the third ball, the green one, out to the left in your left hand, so that it catches the eye of your audience.

● As the yellow ball drops, throw the blue ball up in the air, following a parallel path; and bring the green ball across your body, crossing behind the other two balls. Keep the ball showing in the tips of your fingers.

● Cut the green ball across to your right as shown. The ball, in fact, never leaves your hand, but creates an illusion of movement behind the other two balls.

■ **throw yellow** ▶ **throw, blue, cross green** ▶ **cut green** ▶

● Time the backward and forward movement so that your left hand crosses as the yellow and blue balls are caught and thrown. Here the green ball is moving back across your body to the left.

● The yellow ball is thrown up from your right hand and the falling blue ball is caught. Your left hand moves across your body out to the left.

● At this moment, the hands are apart at waist level as shown. The yellow ball is still in the air, and your eyes are fixed on it. Face slightly to the right to keep your body facing toward the ball.

● As the yellow ball drops, throw the blue ball up on the left side of your body as shown for variation. Pass the green ball across behind the other two as before.

cross green   ▶   **throw, catch, cut back**   ▶   **watch**   ▶   **start over**   ❚❚

three ball columns

This routine is exactly the same as the two ball column shown on pages 22–23, with an additional third ball held and thrown in your left hand. In this sequence, the yellow and green balls are in your right hand, and the blue ball is in your left hand. Make sure that all the balls are thrown vertically into the air and do not cross over. Throw the balls to the same height.

● Start by throwing the first ball from your right hand, the yellow one, straight up in the air. Keep your eyes on the ball facing straight ahead.

● As the first ball starts to drop, throw the blue ball in your left hand into the air, immediately followed by the green ball in your right hand. At this point, all three balls are in the air at once.

● Catch the yellow ball in your right hand and wait for the other two balls, the blue and green, to start dropping. They should both drop close together.

■ throw ▶ throw, throw ▶ catch ▶

● Throw the yellow ball into the air, then catch the green ball in your right hand and the blue ball in your left. This happens almost simultaneously.

● Keep your weight evenly balanced on the balls of your feet with your feet the width of your hips apart. Always concentrate on the ball in the air. The catching and throwing movement will become automatic.

● As the yellow ball drops in its column, the green and blue balls are thrown into the air together. As a variation, the yellow (outer) ball can be thrown at the same time as the blue ball.

● Your hands go up and down to throw and catch the balls. Keep them moving smoothly and easily. You may also find it helps if you bend your knees slightly as you throw and catch to maintain your rhythm and balance.

throw, catch ▶ **watch** ▶ **throw, throw** ▶ **repeat** ❚❚

bounce juggling with balls

As an alternative to juggling in the air, you can juggle on the floor, bouncing the balls in a number of different ways. You need special bouncy balls and a smooth floor. This routine shows bounce juggling in normal cascade style, but you can try a reverse cascade or shower instead. Here the balls are lifted slightly in the air and released, so they fall in front of the opposite foot.

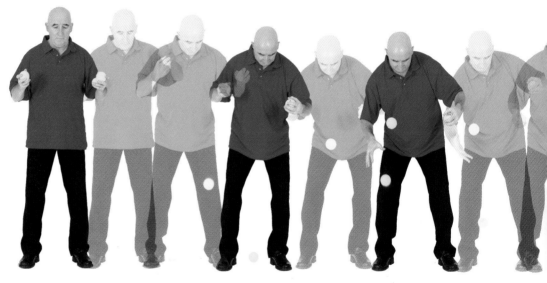

● Start holding two balls in your right hand and one in your left. Stand with your legs shoulder width apart, and your weight evenly on both feet. Bend your knees slightly to help you move from side to side.

● Turn your hand over as you throw the ball to angle the ball in. Aim the first ball so it lands opposite your left foot. As it starts to rise toward you, move your right hand out to throw the second ball.

● As the second ball is thrown, move your right hand down to catch the first ball as shown. Let the ball come easily into the palm of your hand.

■ stand with legs apart ▶ throw one ▶ throw two ▶

● The second ball has been caught in your left hand. As the balls come into your hands, turn the palms over so they face up, and raise your hands so the balls bounce evenly to the correct height.

● In this sequence, a throw has gone astray, and the ball has touched your left foot and bounced up on the wrong side. If your weight is evenly distributed, you can still move quickly enough to make the catch.

● This ball is rising toward your right-hand side. The juggler quickly adjusts his position to throw the ball and then make the catch.

● To end the routine, catch two balls in one hand. As you become more skilled, you can speed up the routine by forcing the balls down onto the floor to make them bounce faster or use the reverse cascade.

catch ‖ **throw** ▶ **throw, catch** ▶ **finish** ‖

three ball shower

The shower is a very different movement from the cascade. Instead of crossing, the balls chase each other around and around in a continuous circle. For most of the time, there are two balls in the air rather than one. It is more difficult to do than the cascade, but some beginners find it easier, because the movement comes more naturally to them.

● Start with two balls, the yellow and orange, in your left hand and throw them up in an arc toward your right hand in quick succession. The balls have to be thrown in a fairly high arc. Look up at the balls in the air.

● The yellow ball is falling toward your right hand, followed by the orange. At this point the red ball is passed from your right hand to your left. This pass is made "blind;" you need to look up the whole time.

● Bring your hands slightly together as you make the pass to reduce the danger of dropping the ball. The yellow ball is caught by your right hand, and you throw the red ball after the orange one with your left hand.

■ **throw** ▶ **throw orange, pass red** ▶ **catch yellow, throw red** ▶

● The red ball moves up toward your left, making a continuous circle from left to right. The yellow ball is passed next and then the orange.

● See how high the orange ball is above your head. This gives you time to pass, catch, and throw the balls. Practice until you can throw each ball in exactly the same arc every time.

● The pass is made with a very small throwing movement. Notice how the juggler turns his hand over to catch the ball. The red ball has just been thrown across and is starting its arc to the right.

● The ball is passed and thrown in an almost continuous movement, with your hands moving inward to make the pass and then out to throw and catch.

throw red ▶ **pass, catch, throw** ▶ **pass yellow, throw red** ▶ **pass, throw catch** ❚❚

underknee throw in cascade

This is a nice piece of trickery that is quite difficult. The important thing is to keep well balanced.

● Start by kneeling down with your left leg out in front to form a rectangular space as shown. Hold two balls, the blue and yellow, in your left hand and the third ball, the green, in your right. Start juggling cascade style.

● Throw the blue ball across to the right. As it descends, throw the green ball to your left. Try to throw the balls in an arc level with your eyes.

● Catch the blue ball as it drops with your right hand, and prepare to throw the yellow ball to the right. The green ball is moving across your body toward your left hand.

● As the green ball starts to drop, the yellow ball is thrown up and across to your right, juggling in the normal cascade style. Make this throw quite high to give yourself time for the underknee move.

 kneel ▶ **throw blue** ▶ **throw green** ▶ **throw yellow** ▶

● At this point, the blue ball, instead of being thrown across to the left, is passed under your knee from right to left. The other two balls are both in the air, crossing each other from left to right and right to left.

● The yellow ball is thrown across to your left, and the green ball is caught in your right hand. As a variation, the blue ball can be thrown under your left leg to your right, making the throw with a flip of your hand as shown.

● The blue ball passes across to your right underneath the yellow ball that is moving left. You will need to practice this underknee throw to achieve the correct trajectory.

● At this point, you are about to throw the green ball to the right. Make the underknee movement on every other rotation of the balls.

mills mess

This is a complicated routine that looks very impressive once it is mastered. It involves throwing the red ball from the wrong side of your body, i.e., with your right hand up past your left shoulder, and the two remaining balls following each other around in a figure-eight pattern. The balls move across your body from side to side and back again.

● Start with the blue and green balls in your left hand and the red ball in your right. Throw the blue ball in the air. It should be thrown to eye level angled slightly toward the right-hand side.

● Take your right arm across your body, and throw the red ball from under your left arm straight up in the air on the left-hand side of your body as shown. Catch the blue ball with your right hand as it falls.

● Throw the green ball with your left hand from the right-hand side of your body. You will need to angle it back across you. Catch the red ball on your right side with your left hand, and bring it back to the left.

■ **throw blue** ▶ **hands across** ▶ **throw green, catch red** ▶

● Throw the blue ball in your right hand toward the left-hand side of your body. In the same motion catch the green ball. The red ball is now thrown from the right-hand side of your body with your left hand.

● This throw is made under your left arm as before, but the other way around. The principle is that the red ball is always thrown up on the outside of your body with the opposite hand, under the arm.

● Your opposite hand moves across your body and then travels back to catch the green or blue ball as they fall. They follow each other, making a figure-eight pattern.

● Always face the front and keep your eyes on the balls in the air. Keep your weight evenly balanced on both feet, and concentrate on building up a rhythm. This routine is not easy and takes time to master.

hands uncross ▶ **throw red** ▶ **hands open** ▶ **repeat** ‖

bouncing on the knee

One way of varying your routine when juggling cascade style is to bounce a ball off various parts of your body. The easiest place to bounce a ball is from the inside of your elbow. Bend your arm slightly and straighten it at the moment of impact. A more spectacular move is to bounce it off your knee, as shown here.

● Start juggling cascade style. The green ball is moving to your right hand, with the orange one crossing it toward the left. The next throw is the blue ball, which you are going to bounce off the top of your right leg.

● In this routine it is important to watch the ball closely as it falls toward you. Hold the other two balls in each hand, and stand on your left leg so you can "knee" the blue ball into the air.

● See how high you need to lift your leg to achieve the necessary impact. The ball bounces up toward you, and as you catch it in your left hand, the orange ball is thrown across your body to the right.

● You can then resume the routine, juggling cascade style as normal. Stand on both feet with your weight evenly distributed.

● Repeat the routine using the blue ball again. If you are equally adept with both legs, you can bounce the ball on your right thigh or bounce it from one leg to the other. This is quite difficult to learn.

● Here the throw is slightly different, and the ball is bounced on your thigh in the center of your body. With practice you can direct it to left or right and use this skill to vary your routine.

● The essence of this trick is to throw accurately, watch the ball carefully, and time the upward movement of your leg so the ball is kneed high into the air. Soccer players will find this move relatively easy!

throw ▶ **bounce blue** ▶ **bounce ball left and right** ▶ **finish**   **11**

bouncing on the head

This is another variation on the cascade style of juggling. It is a lot simpler than it appears at first sight, and once you have become used to throwing the ball accurately onto your head, you will find that you can head balls at will to the right or left.

● Start juggling cascade style with three balls in the normal way. When you want to head a ball, throw it up a bit higher so it travels directly toward the center of your forehead. Watch the ball carefully.

● The blue ball has been thrown up from your right hand. This is the ball you are going to head. The yellow ball is caught in your left hand..

● See how the blue ball lands exactly in the center of your forehead. You can then nod it gently into your left hand. As the blue ball travels to your left, the yellow ball is thrown across to the right in the normal way.

■ **throw blue** ▶ **catch yellow** ▶ **head blue** ▶

● Throw the green ball from your right hand. You are going to head this ball to the left, following the blue. Here the throw is not so accuarate. You can adjust your position by leaning back and to the right.

● The green ball has been nodded onto the left and the blue ball thrown across to the right. In this sequence, every ball is headed in turn, with each throw being made from your right hand.

● It is now the yellow ball's turn. Notice how the juggler keeps his eyes on the ball at all times, watching it carefully onto his forehead. You need to stand with your feet fairly wide apart and shift your weight quickly.

● The green ball has been thrown across to your right and the blue ball thrown up as it arrives. You can head the ball in either direction and head every ball, every second ball, or every third ball. Create your own rhythm.

| head green | ▶ | head, throw | ▶ | head yellow | ▶ | finish | ❚❚ |

catching on your neck

This spectacular variation to juggling cascade style with three balls is a lot easier than it looks. The ball rolls down the back of the neck, and is then trapped in the hollow at the neck's base. To flick the ball back into the air, you have to bend forward and then flick your head up. You can then catch the ball and start juggling cascade style again.

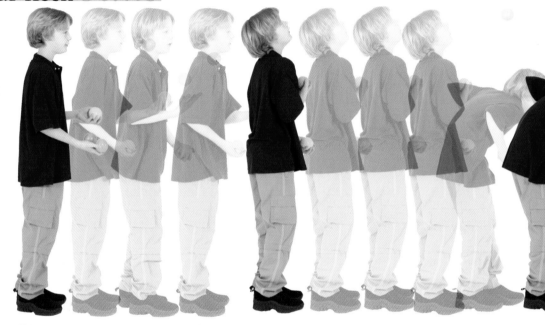

● It is best to practice this routine using just one ball. When you have mastered it, incorporate it into your cascade-style routine using three balls. Catch two balls in your right hand and one in your left.

● Throw the green ball from your right hand into the air and watch it carefully as it comes down. You may have to move slightly to left or right, depending on the accuracy of your throw. Keep your neck relaxed.

● As the ball comes down, bend forward so that it lands on the back of your head. Raise your shoulders to form a cradle for the ball and stay relaxed.

■ **throw** ▶ **watch, relax neck** ▶ **bend forward** ▶

● When the ball is securely trapped, raise your head slightly and the ball will roll down into the hollow at the base of your neck. Hold this position so your audience can see that you have the ball under control.

● When you want to toss the ball back into the air, lower your head and let the ball roll forward. Then, when the ball is steady, flick your head sharply upward.

● The ball will be thrown up off the back of your neck into the air. You will need to practice so you get enough height on the ball that you can stand up straight as the ball passes over your head.

● Catch the ball in your right hand, and start juggling cascade style again. You need to keep well balanced during this routine.

trap the ball   ▶   **lower head**   ▶   **flick up**   ▶   **catch**   ❚❚

head balance and ear roll

This is one of the many variations that you can use in the cascade style routine. You need very good balance and careful control of the balls to succeed. It does need a lot of practice beforehand. Note that it is extremely difficult to do if you have long hair!

● Start by juggling cascade style from hand to hand. Catch two of the balls, and throw the third one straight up so that it lands on your forehead. You may have to bounce it there to get it under control.

● You need to have the ball balanced precisely on your head before you roll it onto your ear. Here the ball is traveling toward your head, and you need to bend backward so the ball comes lightly onto your head.

● Once the ball is motionless on your forehead, it can be rolled onto your ear. To roll it on to your right ear, tilt your head sharply to the left, as shown, slowing the movement as the ball rolls around.

■ **throw** ▶ **bounce on head** ▶ **balance** ▶

● With practice you will be able to bring the ball to a halt balanced on your ear. Notice that your body is leaning well to the left with most of the weight on your left foot. Your knees are bent.

● Use your arms to help maintain your balance, raise your right hand, and let your left hand drop to your waist. Once the ball is stationary, you can flick it back onto your forehead by reversing the previous movement.

● As you do this, bring your back leg forward so your weight is evenly distributed, facing the front with your head tilted back. You will need to use your neck muscles and keep well balanced for this trick.

● To restart your routine, bring your head forward. The ball will be thrown lightly into the air, and you can catch it with your left hand. Then start juggling again.

roll to ear　▶　flick back　▶　back leg forward　▶　nod forward　‖

four ball columns

When you are competent with three ball columns, try four ball columns, juggling two balls in each hand. The principle is the same as two and three ball columns, with the hands moving inward as you catch and throw the balls. Stand with your feet slightly wider apart so you can move easily from side to side if necessary.

● Start by holding two balls in each hand, the orange and yellow balls in your right hand and the red and green balls in your left. Throw the first ball from your right hand, followed by the first ball from your left.

● Throw quickly—one ball after the other—angling each ball slightly toward the center. Here the orange ball is at the top of its arc and has started to drop. Throw the yellow ball into the air along the same path.

● Raise your right hand and catch the orange ball with an inward scoop. The green ball is thrown in the air as the red ball drops.

■ throw, throw ▶ catch, throw ▶ catch, throw ▶

● Let your hand drop as you catch the red ball, and throw the orange ball into the air in quick succession. With practice you will be able to set an easy, regular rhythm with the balls alternately rising and falling.

● The green ball is dropping toward your left hand, and the red ball is just about to be thrown up again. Raise your right hand to catch the yellow ball as it comes down.

● The green ball has dropped into your left hand. The red and yellow balls are both in the air. It is very important to keep your head as still as possible, looking up at the balls in the air.

● The orange ball has just been thrown, and the yellow one is on its way down. The catch and throw movement should be quite automatic. Don't look down at your hands.

catch ▶ **catch, throw** **catch, throw** ▶ **repeat** ❚❚

four ball shower

juggling with balls

This is a spectacular display of juggling, with four balls following each other around in the air, all traveling in the same direction. The balls are thrown in a high arc from your left hand toward your right, and the balls in your right hand are passed across to your left. It requires the kind of dexterity that can only be achieved with regular practice.

● Start off with two balls in each hand, the red and blue balls in your right hand and the green and yellow balls in your left. Throw the two balls in your left hand in an arc toward the right in quick succession.

● The balls need to be thrown high in the air to give you time to catch and throw. When the yellow and green balls are in the air, pass the blue and then the red ball from your right hand to your left.

● Throw these toward your right in the same arc as the first two balls. There are usually three balls in the air at once. The yellow ball is falling to your right hand, which you raise to catch it.

■ **throw yellow** ▶ **throw green** ▶ **throw blue** ▶

● Catch the yellow ball in your right hand and immediately pass it across to your left. Next, catch the green ball as it follows around. Keep your eyes looking up at the balls in the air. The catch and pass are made "blind."

● The balls follow each other around in a circle. Pass the yellow ball to your left, and catch and pass the blue and red balls in exactly the same way.

● There are always at least two, usually three, balls in the air at any one time, following each other. Performing this routine with colored balls, as shown, makes it more interesting.

● Stand with your legs wide apart to move easily back and forth. Your hands move inward to catch the descending balls. The higher you throw the balls, the more time you will have to catch and throw.

catch yellow, throw red ▶ **throw green, catch blue** ▶ **throw blue** ▶ **catch, throw**

four ball alternate columns

Once you have mastered two ball columns, try juggling with four balls at the same time, two in each hand. The principle behind four ball alternate columns is that the hands move alternately up and down so the four balls rise and fall separately, and the different colored balls appear in rotation.

● Start with two balls in each hand, the red and green balls in your right hand and the blue and orange ones in your left. Throw the first ball in your left hand (blue), followed by the first from in right hand, (yellow).

● Move your hands horizontally from side to side to catch and throw the balls. The green ball is thrown up on the inside while the red drops down to your right hand.

● The orange ball is thrown up on the outside of the blue ball as it descends. Raise your hands to catch each ball, and then let it drop in the normal way.

■ **throw blue, throw red** ▶ **throw green** ▶ **throw orange** ▶

● Stand with your feet hip width apart and try to keep evenly balanced and as still as possible. Face the front and look up at the balls in the air. The movement to catch and throw the balls should be automatic.

● Once you have established a good rhythm, you can throw some balls higher than others to vary your routine. Here the blue ball has been thrown higher in the air.

● The orange ball is thrown up on the outside of the blue ball, and the green ball drops on the inside of the red ball.

● The red ball is thrown up, and your hand moves inward to catch the green ball as it drops. Keep a steady rhythm with the balls rising and falling.

catch, throw ▶ catch, throw ▶ throw blue ▶ catch, finish ❚❚

juggling with five balls

Juggling with five balls is difficult and marks the pinnacle of many juggling ambitions. The basic technique is exactly the same as juggling cascade style with three balls. You always have at least three balls in the air at any one time, and you throw in a regular pattern, right, left, right, left, right. This requires considerable practice.

● Hold the green and red ball in your right hand and the blue, yellow, and orange in your left. Rock back and forth to gain momentum for the fast rhythm required. Throw the blue ball first, then the green and yellow.

● Next, throw the red, and lastly the orange. Throw them about 2 feet higher than normal, and quickly one after the other; you should catch the first ball, the blue, just after throwing the fourth ball, the red.

● There are always at least three balls in the air at any one time. Here the green ball, the second one, is at the height of its arc travelling from right to left, followed by the red ball.

■ **throw blue, then green** ▶ **throw yellow** ▶ **throw red, catch blue** ▶

● The red and orange balls cross over, traveling in opposite directions. The red ball is starting to drop toward your left hand while the orange ball reaches the top of its arc.

● The yellow ball has just been thrown to the left, following the blue ball. The red ball has just arrived in your left hand, with the green ball following it. It is essential to keep your eyes on the balls in the air.

● The blue ball has returned to your left hand and the first cycle has been completed from left to right, and back again. Note how the juggler never looks down as he catches the balls.

● The red ball has just been caught in your right hand and is immediately thrown back to the left as the green ball descends. Juggling with five balls is quite fast, and requires a considerable amount of practice to perfect.

prepare to catch red ▶ **throw yellow, catch red** **catch blue** ▶ **catch red, catch green** ‖

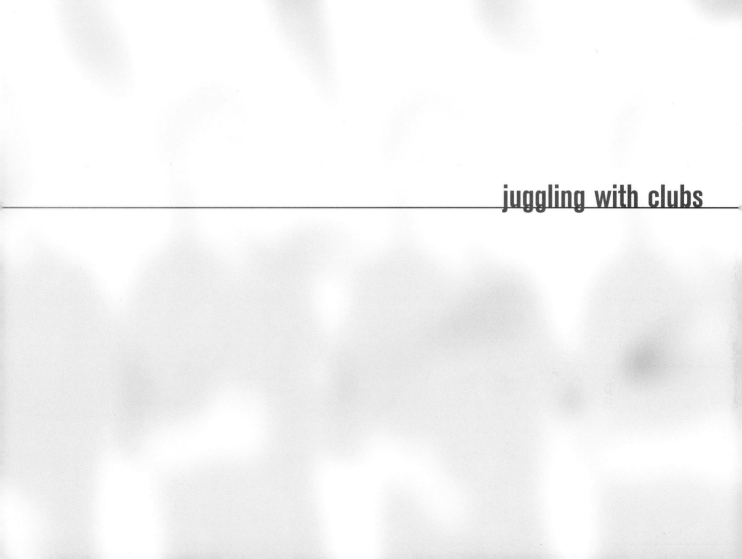

juggling with clubs

one club—hand to hand

This is the first exercise when you start learning to juggle with clubs. It gets you used to the weight and feel of the club, and you learn how much force is needed to throw it into the air and make it spin. Clubs spin naturally, and it only takes a little practice before you can become pretty good.

● Hold one club in your right hand pointing up at a 45 degree angle. Lower your hand a little and then swing it up, letting go of the club when your arm is just about parallel with the ground.

● Angle the club across your body so you can catch it in your left hand. Allow the club to make one spin. You will find that the club will spin naturally.

● Watch the club carefully, and as it rotates and falls toward the left, catch it by the handle in your left hand. The handle of the club should come up just above your head as shown.

● Hold out your left hand and let the handle of the club drop into it, watching it carefully all the time. Let your arm drop as the club falls, so the downward movement of the club is gradual and smooth.

● As you catch the club in your left hand, throw it back to the right immediately. Make sure the throwing movement comes mainly from your arm, not your wrist. Make the throw smoothly and steadily.

● Throw the club up vertically and not too high or forcefully; otherwise, you may have to move your feet to catch it. You should try to keep as still as possible.

● The club is now back in your right hand. Try to get the club traveling the same height and speed on each throw, and make each throw as controlled and consistent as you can. Practice until you are perfect.

two clubs—hand to hand

This is the next stage once you have mastered throwing one club from hand to hand. Throw the clubs from side to side as shown, and, when you are proficient, pause for a beat after the second club. This is the point when the third club will be thrown, once you start juggling cascade style with three clubs. Another exercise is to start with both clubs in one hand and throw them one after the other.

● Start with the clubs in each hand, with your feet slightly apart and your weight evenly balanced. The first club to be thrown is the one in your right hand, the red one. Throw it across to the left.

● Throw the club as shown on pages 54–55. Bring your arm up roughly parallel to the floor, then toss the club in the air across to your left. Give it a turn with your wrist to make it spin once on the way across.

● Notice how high the club is thrown and the way it rotates away from your body. As the red club starts to fall toward the left, bring your left hand up and throw the blue club under the red one across to the right.

| ■ **throw red** | ▶ | **toss, spin** | ▶ | **watch spin, toss blue** | ▶ |

The blue club leaves your hand and passes underneath the red club. You will need to practice throwing two clubs this way to judge the spin accurately and to avoid the clubs "kissing" in midair.

The blue club is at the height of its arc. The thin end of the club is starting to rotate toward your right hand. Notice that the juggler is facing straight ahead and looking up at the club in the air.

Raise your right hand to catch the club as it falls; let it come easily into your hand. Let your hand drop away to absorb the impact.

The clubs are now safely in each hand on the opposite side from the one on which they started. The exercise is then repeated, throwing the club from your right hand, now the blue one, across to the left.

judge spin ▶ **watch** ▶ **catch, drop hand** ▶ **repeat** II

three club cascade

Once you have mastered juggling cascade style with three balls, try the same routine with clubs. Practice with one club first, to get used to throwing it correctly, then move on to two clubs, throwing them from hand to hand. When you are confident you can do this easily, try juggling with three clubs

● Start by holding two clubs in your right hand and one in your left. Hold the top club in your right hand between your thumb and the tips of your fingers. This is the one you throw first. Face the front.

● Throw the yellow club across to your left, making sure it spins once. As it descends, throw the red club across to your right. Keep your eyes on the clubs in the air.

● The last club, the blue one, is thrown from your right hand under the red club as it crosses your body. This movement is exactly the same as juggling cascade style with three balls.

■ **toss yellow** ▶ **toss red** ▶ **toss blue** ▶

● As the blue club crosses to the left, the first club (the yellow one) is thrown back to the right, and the red one is thrown underneath it back to the left.

● Although it may appear much more difficult, once you have mastered the throw, juggling with clubs is easier than juggling with balls because their weight and spin bring the catching end comfortably into your hand.

● The main difficulty that most jugglers have when they start with clubs is avoiding midair collisions. This comes with practice. Count the number of throws you make between drops to monitor your progress.

● The easiest way to finish any routine with three clubs is to hold the first two clubs as shown and then allow the third club to fall on top of the first club in your right hand. Catch it between your thumb and fingers.

two balls and one club

One way of progressing from three balls to three clubs is to introduce the clubs gradually. First try two balls and one club in the cascade pattern. This trick is particularly impressive when the club crosses the balls in midair as the objects are thrown from side to side. Start by holding the two balls in your left hand and the club in your right

● The two balls, the blue and the green, are held in your left hand with the club in your right. Stand with your feet at shoulder's width apart, and your weight distributed evenly on the balls of both feet.

● Throw the first ball, the blue one, in an arc to your right. Bring the club up as the ball peaks, and throw it with one spin to the left. The club passes underneath the ball.

● Catch the blue ball with your right hand, which drops down in the normal way. The club travels across to the left: at this point, the green ball is thrown across to your right. Catch the club in your left hand and let it drop down.

■ **throw blue** ▶ **throw club** ▶ **throw green, catch club** ▶

● The green ball is thrown back to the left and the blue ball to the right. Remember that you will have to adjust to the different weights of the two objects. The club requires more force to throw it across.

● Throw the club across to the left again, and catch the blue ball with your left hand. The club is now traveling to the right and the green ball is thrown back to the left.

● Build up a steady, even rhythm. Make sure you throw the balls higher than the club.

● To finish the routine, hold the club in your right hand and catch both balls in your left. Once you become really proficient, you can throw the club higher, introducing two spins occasionally as a variation.

throw club ▶ **catch blue, throw green** ▶ **build steady rhythm** ▶ **finish** ▮▮

two clubs and one ball

When you have successfully introduced one club, progress to two clubs and one ball. Clubs can bruise the hands of the inexperienced juggler, so it sometimes helps to juggle with gloves on. Once you can do all these routines, ring the changes from three balls, to two balls and one club, then two clubs and one ball, and lastly three clubs.

● Start with two clubs in your right hand and the ball in your left. Stand with your feet shoulder width apart. Hold the club you are throwing first by its end, and the second club in the middle.

● Bring your right arm up and release the first club. Angle it towards your left. The club travels quite high in the air but makes one spin only.

● Watch the club. It has now completed its rotation and is dropping towards your left hand. As it descends throw the ball under it across your body towards the right.

● The ball and club pass each other in the air, travelling in opposite directions. As the ball drops towards your right hand, bring your arm up and throw the second club across to the left along the same arc.

● As the second club drops towards your left hand, throw the first club back towards your right. Try to make each throw as even as possible and keep your weight equally balanced on both feet.

● The ball is thrown from your right hand across to the left. Catch the club in your right hand.

● To finish the routine catch both clubs in your right hand. Hold the first club with the base of your thumb and extend your fingers so that the second club lands on top of the first. This will take practice to perfect.

throw second club ▶ **throw first club** ▶ **throw ball, catch first club** ▶ **catch second club, finish**   II

three clubs over the shoulder

When you can juggle competently with three clubs, try juggling over your shoulder. This is one of the best tricks to include in your routine. Practice by throwing one club from your right hand behind your back, coming over your left shoulder to your left hand. It helps if you lean slightly to the right when you make the throw. Keep the club to a single spin for the time being.

● Start juggling in cascade style with two clubs in your left hand and one in your right. Throw the first club from your left hand, followed by the one in your right as normal. Keep the clubs to a single spin.

● When you have established a good rhythm, prepare to throw the club over your shoulder. You will need to throw the club from your right hand rather higher to allow you time to make the throw behind your back.

● As the second club falls toward your right hand, swing the club in your left hand, the blue one, behind your back, leaning to the left so it can pass over your right shoulder.

■ **throw** ▶ **throw right** ▶ **catch, swing behind** ▶

● The club is swung across your back as shown above. Keep your eyes on the clubs, facing straight to the front.

● The club in your right hand is thrown across to the left in the normal manner, while the blue club, which has been thrown over your shoulder, drops to the right.

● The third club moves across to the left, and your right hand is raised to catch the club coming over your shoulder.

● The routine is now completed, and you can continue to juggle cascade style. With practice you can throw the clubs over each shoulder alternately, or complete the sequence while moving around in a circle.

face front ▶ **over the shoulder** ▶ **catch club over shoulder** ▶ **finish**   II

three clubs under the legs

Once you can juggle cascade style with three clubs, there are a number of tricks you can learn. Throwing the clubs under your legs is one of the simplest and can be managed fairly easily. Other variations include throwing the clubs under each leg alternately; throwing with the right hand under the left leg; and throwing while walking around the room.

● To follow this routine, start with two clubs in your left hand and one in your right. Start juggling cascade style, throwing the first club across to your right in the normal way. The clubs should make one spin only.

● Throw the club from your right hand slightly higher than usual. At the same time drop your left hand and raise your left leg.

● Throw the club under your leg toward the right. Practice so the club is thrown clear of your leg toward the right. You can also hold the club in your right hand out to the side to help your balance.

● Catch the club traveling to the left in your left hand, and throw the next club across to the left underneath the club falling down into your right hand. This is the club you have thrown under your leg.

● You can now repeat the routine, throwing the club the other way under your right leg. The series of movements is exactly the same, but carried out in reverse. Flick your wrist to get the club high enough.

● This time, hold the club in your left hand out to the side to help your balance. The clubs should pass just over the top of your head, as shown, rotating in toward you.

● Finish the routine in the normal way. It is possible to throw under your right leg with your left hand or vice versa. It is even more spectacular to throw alternate clubs under the same leg in different directions.

three clubs with two spins

When you have achieved juggling cascade style with one spin, you can move on to juggling cascade style with two spins. It takes time to learn how to throw and catch the clubs with two spins. Start by throwing the clubs with one spin, then gradually build up to two spins—first with one club, and increasing the frequency as you improve.

● In this routine, start holding two clubs in your left hand and one in your right. The first club is thrown from your left hand across to your right in the normal way.

● Gradually build up the tempo. When you are ready, throw one club higher, giving the club an extra twist with your wrist. It will then spin twice in the air. Catch it in the normal way.

● The rotation of your wrist controls the spin, and the movement of your arm controls the height of the club. The club has been caught in your right hand, with the third club traveling to the left.

● The catch has just been made with your left hand, which drops down. Your right hand comes up to throw the next club. It is then in the correct position to catch the next club as it travels to the right.

● The club thrown from your right hand travels across to the left with a double rotation. Notice how the right hand drops as it makes the next catch.

● Always face straight ahead, and watch the clubs spinning in the air. Keep your weight evenly balanced on both feet and move from side to side as necessary. The more experienced you are, the less you have to move.

● The routine ends in the normal way, with two clubs being caught in one hand (in this case, the left) while the third club is held in the right.

second spin ▶ **double rotation** ▶ **face straight ahead** ▶ **catch, finish** ‖

placing a club between your legs

You can make this part of your routine, and it is effective when you stop juggling and pretend to the audience that you don't know where the third club has gone. It is even more spectacular when it is done with fire clubs, with the burning end placed behind you, although you need to be very proficient before you attempt this routine.

● Stand with your feet hip width apart. Hold two clubs in your left hand and one in your right. Start to juggle cascade style in the normal way.

● When you have established a good rhythm, throw the club from your right hand toward your left rather higher than normal. This allows you time to place the club in your left hand between your legs as shown.

● Continue juggling cascade style, throwing the two remaining clubs from hand to hand. Throw the blue club from your right hand a bit higher than normal as the yellow club falls to your right.

● Catch the yellow club in your left hand, and at the same time pull the red club out from between your legs with your right hand. The yellow club is then thrown back to the right.

● Your left hand is raised to catch the blue club as it falls, and the red club is pulled free and thrown into the air in virtually the same movement. It follows the yellow club across to your right.

● Catch the yellow club in your right hand, and throw it back to the left. In the sequence above, the blue club is about to be thrown across to the left, while the red club falls into your right hand.

● To finish the routine, hold two clubs (one in each hand), and let the last club come down into your right hand. It will smack on top of the first club. Tuck the first club under the base of your thumb and extend your fingers.

pull club out ▶ **raise hand, catch blue** ▶ **catch yellow, throw** ▶ **finish** ‖

four clubs and two spins

The principle behind juggling with four clubs is exactly the same as juggling with four balls, although it looks a good deal more complicated. The clubs travel up and down in columns and do not cross over. The two clubs in the right hand are purple, while the two in the left are white with a purple band.

● Stand facing the front holding two clubs in each hand. You can throw the clubs so they rise and fall in unison, but here the first throw is made from the left hand with the club traveling on the outside.

● The next club thrown is the first club from your right hand. It, too, travels up on the outside. You need to throw the clubs quite high in the air so they have time to spin twice before you catch them.

● The first club has fallen toward your left hand, and the next club is thrown up on the inside path. Your hand moves back and forth along the horizontal plane to catch and throw the clubs.

■ **throw left** ▶ **throw right** ▶ **watch spins** ▶

● The clubs will rise and fall in sequence. In the picture above, the club in your right hand has been thrown up on the inside track, with your hand moving out to catch the one falling on the outside.

● The club in your left hand is thrown up on the inside, and the outer club falls toward you. The club in your right hand is about to be thrown. Notice how each hand rises to throw and then catch the descending club.

● Practice with two clubs in each hand to start with, then try four clubs when you feel confident you can master throwing and catching. It is more difficult to avoid midair collisions with four clubs.

● The best way to finish is to catch two clubs in your right hand and then throw the last club much higher with a triple spin. This gives you time to transfer the third club to the right and then catch the last club with your left.

move hand out ▶ **throw, catch** ▶ **two clubs, then four** ▶ **catch, finish** II

passing clubs *juggling with clubs*

You need to be able to juggle competently with three clubs in cascade style before attempting to pass clubs to a partner. Keep your eye on your partner's clubs as well as your own.

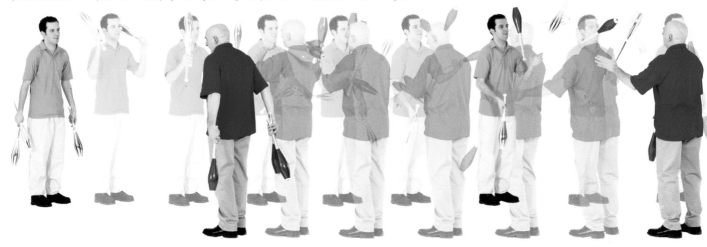

● Start facing your partner standing about 6 feet apart. Hold two clubs in your right hand and one in your left. Raise your clubs over your shoulders to signal the start of the routine. Then start juggling cascade style.

● It is important that you both start juggling at the same moment and establish the same rhythm. Stand with your feet apart and your left foot slightly forward.

● As you both bring your hands down, immediately pass from your right hand to your partner's left. Count each club as it leaves your right hand, and throw every second club across to your partner's left hand.

● Each throw has to be accurate. Drop your right hand lower than normal and then bring your arm up until it is almost parallel with the ground. The throw is made with the minimum of wrist action.

■ **raise club**　　　　　**establish rhythm**　▶　**throw**　　　▶　**catch, throw**　　　▶

● The club travels across to your partner's left, making one revolution, and is caught with the handle pointing down. The blue club is just about to be thrown toward the right-hand juggler.

● The throws are made simultaneously from the right hand. Once the catch has been made, the left hand moves in an outside sweep, and the juggling continues in normal cascade style.

● When you are very skilled, the passes can be made every time from your right hand. This is what is happening here, with the clubs being thrown across from one juggler to another in a constant stream.

● You can incorporate a number of tricks into this routine, such as double spin passes, and throws under the leg and behind the back. You can even juggle with three people, although the timing must be absolutely perfect.

catch, handle down ▶ **throw** ▶ **pass** ▶ **finish** II

juggling with other objects

juggling with fruit

juggling with other objects

As you become more experienced, you can experiment by juggling with a number of different items. One of the easiest is fruit: you can start with apples and oranges that are the same shape and weight. In this sequence, the juggler has chosen a banana as one of the fruits, and to make it more difficult, he is juggling the banana with two spins as it rises and falls.

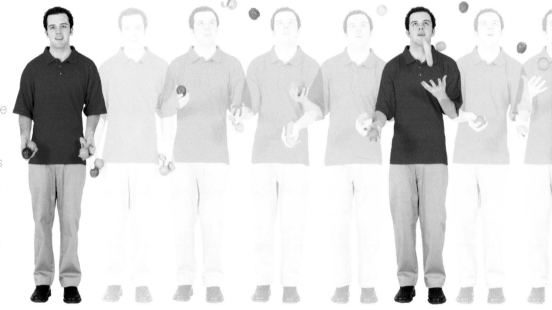

● Start with two pieces of fruit in each hand, juggling in columns. The juggler has chosen a red apple and an orange in his right hand, and a green apple and a banana in his left, which provides good color contrast.

● Stand facing the front with your weight evenly balanced on both feet. Start with the left-hand column, throwing the green apple into the air first, and then followed by the red apple. Throw all the fruit fairly high.

● As the green apple falls, throw the banana into the air on the inside. Your hand will move out along a horizontal plane to catch the apple. Flick the banana into the air to make it spin. All the fruit is rising and falling vertically.

■ toss apples   ▶   face front, weight balanced   ▶   toss banana   ▶

● Your right hand moves in to throw the green apple and then out to catch the banana. Your left hand moves out to throw the orange and then in to catch the red apple. Keep looking straight up at the fruit in the air.

● Throw the red apple into the air as the orange falls down. Keep an even, steady rhythm. You will need to practice with different types of fruit so they can all be thrown to the same height.

● Throw the banana and catch the green apple; throw the orange and then catch the red apple. Juggling in columns is attractive—the objects follow each other into the air in rapid succession like a colored fountain.

● Finish by catching all the fruit in each hand. Juggling with fruit is easiest, if you choose fruit that is fairly hard and can easily be thrown into the air and caught. Soft, overripe fruit is not suitable, particularly if you drop it!

hat trick 1

Jugglers and conjurors entertain audiences in various ways. The common thread is manual dexterity and physical coordination. Many routines are borrowed from street artists, and juggling with hats is one of them. This trick is fairly easy to learn, and is also a good opportunity to find a use for an old bowler hat.

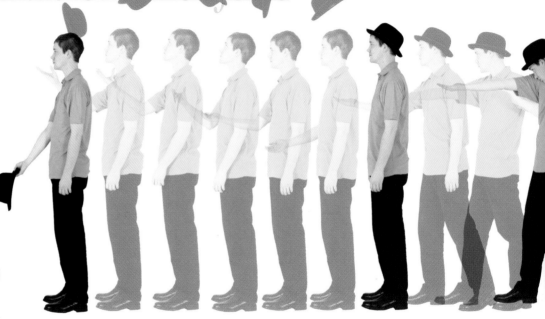

● Stand with your feet hip width apart. Hold your hat out in front of you, with your fingers underneath the brim and your thumb on top. It doesn't have to be a bowler, but it helps if it has a firm brim.

● Flip the hat up in front of you so that it makes a complete revolution in the air. Release the hat when your arm is just about parallel to the floor.

● The hat spins toward you, and as it completes its turn, it should settle on your head. Keep watching the hat carefully and bend your knees to catch it with your head. You may also have to lean your neck slightly forward.

■ **throw hat** ▶ **spin** ▶ **catch on head** ▶

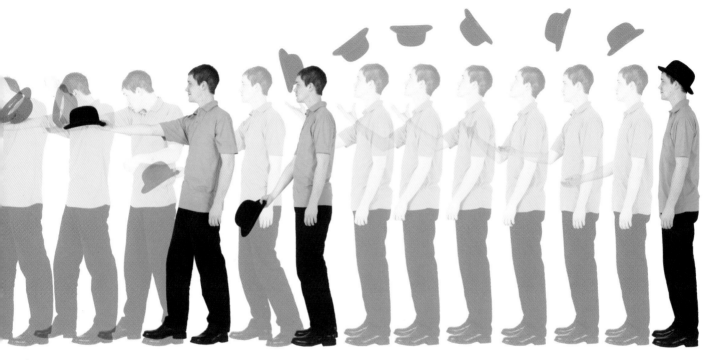

● Once the hat is on your head, move your left leg back one pace as shown. Stretch your right arm straight out, palm up, and parallel to the floor; and put your left arm behind your neck with your elbow pointing out.

● Tilt your chin down and look down toward your right hand; then roll the hat off your head and down your right arm. It should end up clasped in your right hand with your fingers under the brim as before.

● As the hat travels down your arm, take your left hand back beside your body, and move your left leg back so you are standing evenly on both feet, facing the front.

● You are now in a position to repeat the sequence. It does require a good deal of practice to get the hat correctly on your head at each throw, but it is very satisfying when you have mastered it.

remove hat ▶ **roll hat** ▶ **stand evenly** ▶ **finish** **ll**

hat trick 2

This is a more spectacular trick using three hats. Ideally, they should be different sorts of hats, but bowlers or tophats with hard rims are most easily thrown and caught. All the hats you use should fit properly on your head.

● This routine has similarities to juggling in a shower pattern, using your head as a staging post and completing the movements with your arms. It looks spectacular when done with rhythm and panache.

● Start with one hat on your head and one in each of your hands. Bring your left arm up and throw the hat in a floating motion across the top of your head to your right.

● Continue the movement of your hand and take off the hat on your head: do this smoothly isn one motion. Put the hat in your right hand on your head and then catch the first hat as it goes over your head.

■ **toss hat**　　▶　　**remove hat**　　▶　　**catch**　　▶

● You have just placed the third hat, the top hat, on your head. Your right hand drops down to catch the rim of the bowler as it falls.

● The movement is repeated with the bowler in your left hand thrown across your head. You need to stand with one foot in front of the other, with knees bent, to enable you to move from side to side.

● The top hat is doffed and is replaced by a bowler. You will have to be fairly quick and deft to get these movements correct. You always throw and remove the hat on your head with your left hand.

● You put the new hat on your head and catch with your right. The more you practice and the faster you can perform this trick, the more it will look as if the hats are changing places without any effort on your part.

toss hat ▶ repeat ▶ catch ▶ finish ‖

spinning plates

This is one of those juggling tricks that looks impossible to perform, but is actually fairly easy. You will need to use specially formed plastic plates and spinning sticks, which are available from juggling suppliers.

● Start with one plate held vertically on the spinning stick in your right hand with the other plate and stick in your left. Start the plate spinning fairly slowly, making large circles. Keep your arm still and spin with your wrist.

● Gradually build up speed. As the plate spins around faster and faster, you will be able to move the stick in to the center of the plate. You can then hold the plate upright, and it will spin around on its stick by itself.

● Move the first plate and stick across so you can hold it in your left hand. At this point, you are holding the green plate and its stick, as well as the yellow plate, in your left hand. The second stick is in your right hand.

■ **spin green** ▶ **center stick** ▶ **transfer hand** ▶

● Holding the green plate out to the right, start the yellow plate spinning in the same way as the green plate. Gradually build up speed until both plates are spinning horizontally.

● Keep one plate above the other to avoid knocking them together in midair. If the plates start to slow down, you can spin them again to rebuild their momentum.

● A good party trick is to hold both sticks in your mouth. Tilt your head back and put the stick in your right hand into your mouth, followed by the one in your left. Hold onto the sticks until you have got them balanced.

● Hold the sticks with your back teeth and be careful. Take your hands away and the plates continue spinning. Keep your eyes on the plates, and as they start to slow down, you can take the sticks away.

start yellow ▶ **keep plates above each other** ▶ **transfer to mouth** ▶ **finish** ❚❚

Juggling with cigar boxes introduces a different element into the juggler's routine. You can convert your own cigar boxes, but it is easier to buy them from a specialized juggling or magic supplier. These boxes have been specially reinforced with strips of suede that are glued down the sides, making them easier to handle and catch.

● Hold the three boxes in a line as shown—the blue box in your right hand, the yellow box in your left, and the red box held by pressure from the other two. Hold the boxes with your fingers in front and thumbs behind.

● The object of the trick is to turn the box in your right hand 180 degrees and back again, trapping the red box on each turn.

● Lift the line of boxes quickly into the air, and turn your right hand 180 degrees.

● Snap the boxes together, trapping the red box in the middle. You will need to bend down and drop your arms to trap the box before it falls to the ground. When the boxes are firmly in line, stand up straight.

● As you rise, lift the boxes into the air again and turn your right hand counterclockwise back to its original position.

● Snap the boxes together to trap them in line. It is easier to catch them with both hands on top of the outer boxes, and you should not have to bend down so far.

● Repeat the routine, building up speed and rhythm. Snap the boxes together and concentrate on the middle box. Stand with your feet shoulder width apart and bend up and down with your knees.

snap together ▶ **lift boxes** ▶ **snap together** ▶ **repeat** ‖

cigar boxes 2

juggling with other objects

This is a more advanced trick that requires speed and agility. In addition to the routines shown here and on pages 86–87, jugglers can learn other cigar-box routines, the most spectacular being the balancing routines using nine boxes. As with all juggling, start with the simple moves, then work your way up as you improve.

● In this routine, the red box in your left hand is released, and you catch the center yellow box. This is then quickly moved to the outside of the line, and the three boxes are then trapped before they touch the floor.

● Bend forward slightly at the knees and then straighten to help you lift the boxes into the air. This movement must be quick and sharp, but must also be controlled.

● Let go of the outer box, the red one, with your left hand, and catch the central yellow box. Keep the boxes far enough in front of you so you do not knock the red box with your elbow as you do this.

● Bring the blue and yellow boxes down and out to the side as shown. You will need to turn slightly to the left to allow the red box to fall evenly between the two outer boxes.

● Concentrate on the central box, and bring the two outer boxes together. If the center box tilts, as it has here, you will need to adjust the angle of the outer boxes to make a straight line.

● Notice the concentration on the center box. The line is almost complete, and the three boxes are then snapped together.

● Once the boxes are in line, bring them back into the horizontal plane, if necessary, and repeat the routine. Keep your knees flexible, and move up and down with the boxes as you build up a rhythm.

juggling an umbrella

This makes an excellent party trick. You need to use a long umbrella which, ideally, should be made of wood. Stand back from the audience in case of accidents.

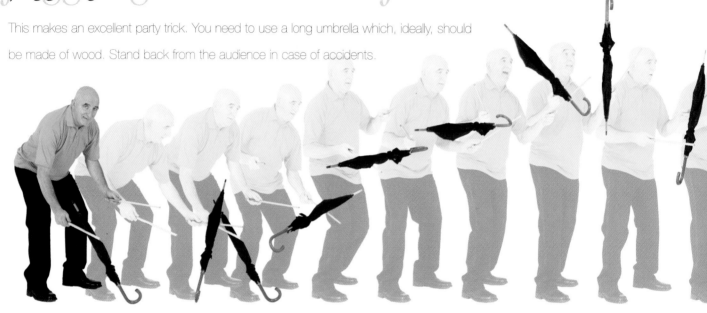

● Start with the umbrella resting handle-down on the floor and leaning against one of your juggling sticks.

● Push it across to the other stick, then bat it back and forth, as you gradually build up momentum. Try to hit the umbrella just above the middle. As the speed builds up, you can raise the umbrella off the floor.

● Keep the umbrella at waist level using a sharp rat-a-tat rhythm. The juggling sticks should be hitting the umbrella in the same spot, if you can.

● As a finale, you can make the umbrella spin in the air, passing it from one stick to the other. Lift the umbrella sharply with your right stick to impart the spin, rotating it in an counterclockwise direction.

■ **rest umbrella** ▶ **push, bat** ▶ **raise** ▶ **start the turn** ▶

● You need to toss the umbrella fairly high to allow it to turn. As it falls toward your left stick, flick it back to the right.

● Try to hit the umbrella when it is at an angle to the ground, because this means you to toss it from side to side more easily. Notice that the handle of the umbrella remains uppermost for stability.

● When you want to finish, adjust the position of your juggling stick in your left hand so you are holding it in the middle. Let the umbrella fall horizontally toward this hand.

● Catch the umbrella in your left hand. With practice you will find that you can hold onto the stick and catch the umbrella at the same time.

return ▶ **toss, side to side** ▶ **complete the turn** ▶ **catch, finish** **II**

three plates

Juggling with three plates in cascade style is very similar to juggling with three balls. The plates are held, two in one hand, one in another, and one thrown from side to side. The main difference is that they have to be caught by the rim between the thumb and index finger. Stand with your feet apart, leaning slightly forward for balance.

● Start with two plates, the yellow and green ones, in your left hand, and the blue plate in your right. Make the first throw with your left hand toward the right. Throw the plates so they are in a vertical position as shown.

● Hold onto the yellow plate with your left hand, and as the green plate comes down to your right, throw the blue plate across to the left.

● Catch the green plate in your right hand, reaching up as it descends. The green and blue plates will pass each other in the air.

■ **throw** **throw** ▶ **catch and throw** ▶

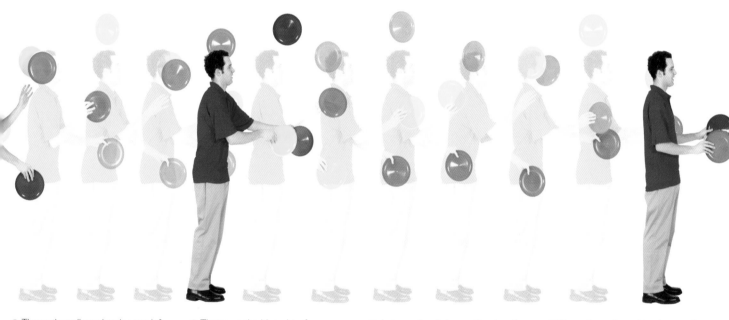

● Throw the yellow plate in your left hand up past the blue plate as it descends toward you. Throw the green plate from right to left.

● Throw up the blue plate from your left hand; catch the yellow plate in your right hand. Prepare to throw the yellow plate from your right hand, and catch the green in your left as it comes down toward you.

● Let your hand drop as the rim of the plate comes into it. This will help you to maintain an even rhythm. Throw the plates fairly high and remember to hold them firmly, keeping your arms moving all the time.

● Throw the yellow plate, then catch the blue, then the yellow to finish. You will need to practice throwing the plates so that they maintain a vertical plane.

throw, catch, throw ▶ **throw, catch** ▶ **throw, catch** ▶ **finish** ❚❚

index